T0273822

Daily Wisdom

Sayings of the Prophet Muhammad

Daily Wisdom

Sayings of the Prophet Muhammad

There is an excellent example (of conduct)
for you in Prophet Muhammad,
the Messenger of God.

The Qur'an 33:21

Daily Wisdom: Sayings of the Prophet Muhammad

First published in England by

Kube Publishing Ltd
Markfield Conference Centre
Ratby Lane, Markfield,
Leicestershire LE67 9SY
United Kingdom

Tel: +44 (0) 1530 249230
Fax: +44 (0) 1530 249656

Website: www.kubepublishing.com
Email: info@kubepublishing.com

Originally published in India as
365 Sayings of the Prophet
Jaico, 2008.

18th Impression, 2024

Cataloguing-in-Publication Data
is available from the British Library

ISBN 978-1-84774-018-2 casebound
ISBN 978-1-84774-022-9 casebound (boxed deluxe edition)

Book design & typesetting
Imtiaze Ahmed

Printed by: Imak Ofset - Turkey

CONTENTS

KEY TO ABBREVIATIONS

The following abbreviations have been used in the present work to indicate the various sources of the Prophet's Sayings. Reference is made to the compilers or titles of major collections of *Hadith* (the Prophet's Sayings), and other abbreviations are also included:

A = Ahmad
AM = *al-Adab al-Mufrad* of al-Bukhari
B = Bukhari
b. = ibn or bin, 'son of'
BQ = Bayhaqi
D = Abu Dawud
H = Hakim
I = Ibn Majah
JS = *al-Jami' al-Saghir* of al-Suyuti
KA = *Kitab al-Adhkar* of al-Nawawi
KU = *Kanz al-Ummal* of Ali al-Muttaqi
M = Muslim
MK = Malik
MSH = *Mishkat al-Masabih* of al-Khatib al-Tabrizi
N = Nasa'i
R = Razin
RS = *Riyadh al-Salihin* of al-Nawawi
SS = *Sharh al-Sunnah* of al-Baghawi
T = Tirmidhi
TA = *Tuhfa al-Ahwazi* of al-Mubarakfuri
TB = Tabarani
TT = *Targhib wa'l-Tarhib* of al-Mundhiri

PREFACE

The present work seeks to familiarize readers with one of the primary sources of Islamic faith and practice, the *Hadith* (Prophet Muhammad's Sayings). His Sayings, reflecting profound wisdom and morality, have been one of the main sources of guidance and law for Muslims around the world from the early days of Islam up to the present time. His Sayings represent the elaboration of the truths contained in the Qur'an, the Word of God revealed to Prophet Muhammd ﷺ. It is therefore not surprising that a principle alluded to in the Qur'an is explained further in the Prophet's Sayings. Likewise, some of the Qur'anic precepts are articulated in various ways in his Sayings. The early Muslims fully recognized the Prophet's role in the Divine scheme of things, for he helped them see and follow the Way prescribed by God to earn His pleasure, which, in turn, brought to them abiding success in both the worlds. Since the Prophet ﷺ was their role model, and continues to be so up to this day, they tried their best to emulate him. Their relationship with him is captured by the following account:

> All his actions served them as a precedent (*Sunnah*), every word falling from his lips to them, and all his actions were virtuous in their eyes, which they wanted to follow as faithfully as they could. When he chose a gold ring for himself, his friends also put it on; when he put it off, they threw it away, and put on a silver ring instead, following his example. If he offered prayers at midnight, all his friends wanted to do the same, and he had to stop them from doing so as well. If he fasted continuously for more

> than a day, his followers also desired to do the same, and he had to explain to them his special privileges. Zayd b. Khalid spent one whole night at his door in order to see him offer his night prayers. Nawwas b. Sam'an stayed at Madinah for one whole year in order to enquire from him what was virtue and what was wrongdoing. Abu Sa'id al-Khudri observed keenly how long he kept standing in his afternoon prayers. Ibn 'Umar counted how many times he asked for the pardon of God in one sitting.

Moreover, apart from conveying the Divine message, as a social reformer and spiritual mentor *par excellence*, Muhammad ﷺ brought about the moral and spiritual transformation of the first generation of believers. Throughout his Prophetic career, he instructed them day and night in every walk of life, illustrating what should be done and what should be avoided. It went a long way towards instilling the conviction among his followers that all of their acts, both what they did or failed to do, no matter how trivial these might have seemed to them, were closely watched by God. These early Muslims and those that came after them took every possible step to record all the teachings of the Prophet ﷺ, which came to constitute the corpus of *Hadith*.

Another purpose of this selection is to help readers gain or renew their acquaintance with Prophet Muhammad ﷺ, whom Muslims view as the most inspiring figure in history, who influenced human thought and life, and whose career stands out for his astounding success. His Sayings on a wide range of topics and issues, as recorded in this work, provide a glimpse of his mind and character – his overflowing love and affection for humanity, especially for the weak, the poor, orphans and women; his commitment to fairness and social justice for all; his modesty and simplicity, reflected in his repeated directives that he not be idolized or extolled, as he took great pride in being only a servant of God; and, above all, his ardent desire to promote true faith, high morals and manners and excellent conduct.

This selection of the Prophet's Sayings aims to outline the Islamic worldview, presenting a conspectus of the Islamic code of conduct governing every Muslim's familial, social, political, economic and spiritual life. Non-Muslims may find it a useful introduction to both Islamic faith and practice. Throughout this work, the focus is on illustrating the Prophet's guidelines for leading life as individuals and communities. Some of his teachings are inevitably specific to the Muslim community, such as those that deal with the articles of Islamic faith and the Hereafter. Strikingly enough, most of his teachings are marked by a broad, general outlook, asking Muslims to lead their lives as part of a wider community of men and women, whom, irrespective of their faith, are all servants and creatures of the One True God. Equally valid and relevant is the Prophet's wisdom for non-Muslims as well. Any reader who is not of the Islamic faith will be struck by the

Prophet's universal message and his sincere, genuine concern for the welfare and happiness of humanity at large.

Apart from setting out the Islamic worldview, as reflected in the Prophet's Sayings, it is hoped that the present work will serve as a useful volume for reflection, for soul searching and for self-development. As a single *Hadith* appears on each of its 365 pages, it has been designed to engage readers in a few moments of daily self-reflection throughout the year. Such self-reflection, Muslims believe, is best undertaken in the spirit of striving as far as possible to act on Prophet's teachings, as the way to attain success both in this world and the Hereafter.

This work had originally appeared under the title *365 Sayings of the Prophet Muhammad* and was published by Jaico of Mumbai, India. I am grateful to Mr R.H. Sharma for having given permission to Kube Publishing to bring out the former as a revised version under the present title. I must thank Yahya Birt of Kube Publishing for his valuable editorial suggestions. While every care has been taken to present a largely faithful translation of the Prophet's Sayings from the original Arabic, some of these appear in somewhat abridged form. At times, the import of his Sayings has been paraphrased without deviating considerably from the wording of the original text.

Non-Muslim readers may wish to note that while pronouncing or writing the name of the Prophet Muhammad, Muslims use the honorific formula "may God bless him and give him peace" (which is marked in Arabic as ﷺ in the text). The same norm is followed in this book. Any suggestion to improve this book is highly welcome.

Abdur Raheem Kidwai
Aligarh Muslim University, India
July 2009

INTRODUCTION

In the Islamic scheme of things, the Prophet Muhammad ﷺ occupies a pivotal position. It is one of the essential articles of faith for Muslims to believe in and abide by all that the Prophet ﷺ said or did. His acts and sayings, referred to in Islamic terminology as *Sunnah* and *Hadith* respectively, are, therefore, of great importance and relevance for Muslims in all times and places. The esteem in which Muslims hold the Prophet ﷺ does not hinge upon idolizing him. Rather, they cannot profess or practise Islam without drawing upon the example set by the Prophet ﷺ. The following account brings into sharper focus the significance of the Prophet's Sayings in the broader world context of Islam.

According to the Qur'an, the Islamic Scripture, God sent the Prophet Muhammad ﷺ to teach "the Book and wisdom" (al-Jumu'ah 62:2). At another place, the Qur'an outlines his role: "God has sent down this Reminder (the Qur'an) upon you that you may elucidate to the people the teaching that has been sent down for them" (al-Nahl 16: 44). The same truth is pressed home thus: "We sent among you a Messenger of yourselves, who recites to you our signs, purifies you, instructs you in the Book and in wisdom, and teaches you what you did not know" (al-Baqarah 2: 151). It is not therefore surprising that on being asked to spell out the Prophet's conduct, 'A'ishah, his wife, readily answered that his everyday life demonstrated what the Qur'an taught. The Islamic modes of worship, moral code, socio-political ideals, habits of thought, concern for the Hereafter and spiritual outlook were practised by the Prophet ﷺ, and he served as a living role model for the early Muslims who came to know of or hear about him.

The Qur'an contains several directives urging Muslims to be kind to orphans, the poor, the elderly, women and children. However, they imbibed this moral lesson in the real sense on observing firsthand the Prophet's overflowing love and affection for the downtrodden of society. They saw with their own eyes that he used to skip meals in order to feed the needy. He led a frugal life while he generously helped the poor and the weak. Never did he hit nor take revenge against anyone, though he was persecuted for years. They noted with amazement how he spent his time on visiting the sick, attending funerals and consoling those in distress. As a father, husband and neighbour, he showed them how to perform these basic familial and social roles. His example in real-life situations was closely observed and followed faithfully by his companions. Most importantly, they taught subsequent generations to do the same. This explains why the Prophet's Sayings carry the pride of place in the Islamic worldview.

Another instance in point is afforded by the Qur'anic command for liturgical prayer, which underscores his central role in things Islamic. The Qur'an obliges every Muslim to offer daily prayers. However, it was the Prophet ﷺ who illustrated all aspects of this command: time, place, number, ritual, and way of offering the prayer. Through his example, the Muslims realized the effectiveness of prayer in moulding their outlook on life. His Sayings thus set the agenda for professing and practising Islam.

Of all the Messengers of God, the Prophet Muhammad ﷺ holds the distinction of being the last and final bearer of God's guidance for mankind. More significantly, he is the only Messenger whose entire prophetic career is meticulously preserved in writing. All that he said, did, approved or disapproved of, even with the slightest gesture, is recorded. From the beginning of his Prophetic call, a host of his followers fully devoted themselves to recording and transmitting faithfully his Sayings for posterity. With the passage of time this exercise gained in depth and grounding. The *Hadith* sciences soon developed into one of the most extensive branches of learning in the Islamic tradition. Some of the best Muslim minds collected, edited and promoted *Hadith* studies. This trend continues up to this day, and has contributed much to the popularity and importance of the Prophet's Sayings among Muslims across the world.

Muslims believe that the Prophet ﷺ was constantly under God's care and supervision in discharging his

Prophetic duty, and was inspired and guided by God in all of his acts. Accordingly Muslims are obliged to abide by his teachings, besides those ordained by the Qur'an. The Divine revelation constitutes what we know as the Qur'an, whereas the special knowledge imparted to the Prophet ﷺ by God, which is reflected in his acts and sayings, represents what the Qur'an names as "wisdom". Imparting wisdom is specifically and recurrently mentioned in the Qur'an as the Prophet's main assignment: "God has revealed to you the Book and wisdom, and He taught you what you did not know." (al-Nisa' 4:113).

Elsewhere, the Prophet's family members are reminded of the Divine favours bestowed upon them: "Remember the signs of God and the words of wisdom which are rehearsed in your homes" (al-Ahzab 33:34). "Wisdom" in this verse instance signifies the Prophet's words and deeds. It also explains why it is so important to learn about and act upon the Prophet's Sayings.

God in the Qur'an both sanctions and sanctifies the Prophet's Way in this proclamation:

> As for him who sets himself against the Prophet and follows a path other than that of the believers even after true guidance has become clear to him, God will let him go the way he has turned to, and will cast him into Hell – an evil destination.
>
> (Al-Nisa' 4:115)

Numerous instances in early Islamic history corroborate the point that Muslim rulers were guided by the Prophet's Rulings and Sayings in deciding any matter. It is on record that the Caliph Abu Bakr asked publicly about asked the Prophet's Precedent on any issue that was not in his knowledge. On coming to know what it was, he decided the matter accordingly. The same holds true for Muslim rulers and peoples of later times. They sought and still seek to live by the Prophet's teachings in all aspects of their life. This is the enduring significance and relevance of his Sayings in the lives of more than one billion Muslims around the world today.

Among the many collections of the Prophet's Sayings, edited assiduously by several scholars in the early history of Islam, the following deserve mention. Those interested in the subject would find their study rewarding:

Bukhari's *al-Jami' al-Sahih*

Abu 'Abdullah b. Isma'il al-Bukhari (810-870), of Persian descent, was born in Bukhara, now in Central Asia. God had blessed him with a strong intellect and a sharp retentive memory which contributed much to his later fame as one of the foremost *Hadith* scholars. In his forty-year-long search collecting the Sayings of the Prophet ﷺ, he visited almost all the important centres of Islamic learning in different parts of the

Muslim world. For example, he stayed at Basra for five years, in Hijaz, part of the present-day Saudi Arabia for six years, and travelled several times to Egypt, Kufa and Baghdad. The fruits of his diligent scholarship are collected in his *Sahih al-Bukhari*, containing his careful selection of 7275 thematically arranged Sayings of the Prophet ﷺ. These are sub-divided into 100 sections and 3450 chapters.

Muslim's *Sahih*

Sahih Muslim, another major *Hadith* collection by Abu Husain Asakir Muslim b. Hajjaj (817-874), is second in rank to Bukhari's *Sahih*. Muslim was born in Nishapur and travelled widely in Persia, Iraq, Syria and Egypt to master the discipline of *Hadith*. After examining a large number of the Sayings, he finally selected 4000 authentic reports which feature in his collection.

Abu Dawud's *Sunan*

Abu Dawud Sulayman b. al-Ashtah (817-888) of Arab stock was most probably born in Basra. He pursued the study of *Hadith* in Arabia, Persia, Syria and Egypt and tried to gather all the reported Sayings of the Prophet ﷺ. His collection, *Sunan*, retains the meticulous standards of scholarship found in the works of Bukhari and Muslim. However, his collection also includes some reports that are regarded as unreliable by some scholars. Nonetheless, Abu Dawud does well in pointing out the defects in such reports.

Tirmidhi's *Jami'*

As an illustrious student of Abu Dawud, Abu 'Isa Muhammad b. 'Isa (821-892) carried further the work of his teacher and spiritual master. He also learnt *Hadith* at the feet of Bukhari and Muslim. His labelling of reports as genuine or otherwise is one of the most valuable aspects of his work.

Nasa'i's *Sunan*

Abu 'Abd al-Rahman Ahmad b. Shu'ayb al-Nasa'i (827-915) hailed from Khurasan. He studied *Hadith* in Central Asia and visited Egypt and Syria to collect *Hadith*. His *Sunan*, a large collection of the Prophet's Sayings, is one of the six standard works on the subject. A striking feature of this work is that it contains variants of many Hadith reports, followed by Nasa'i's comments on the authenticity or otherwise of each report.

Ibn Maja's *Sunan*

Abu 'Abdullah Muhammad b. Yazid, popularly known as Ibn Maja (822- 887), was born at Qazwin in Persia. To gain a thorough knowledge of *Hadith*, he visited Persia, Iraq, Syria, Arabia and Egypt. Contained in his collection are 4000 Sayings of the Prophet ﷺ divided into 32 sections and 1500 chapters.

Bayhaqi's *Sunan*

Abu Bakr Ahmad b. al-Husain of Nishapur, popularly known as Bayhaqi (994-1066), learnt *Hadith* at the feet of many eminent scholars. His *Sunan* stands out for its thematic arrangement and its method of evaluating *Hadith* reports.

Malik's *Muwatta'*

Malik b. Anas (711-795) stands out as a distinguished jurist and *Hadith* scholar of Madina in the Arabia peninsula. His collection of *Hadith*, *Muwatta'* also contains the rulings of Madinan jurists. His work is one of the earliest extant writings on *Hadith* and jurisprudence.

Select Bibliography

Those interested in further study may find this select bibliography of English-language references useful.

Contemporary Selections of the Prophet's Sayings

Ahmad, Ghazi, *Sayings of the Prophet Muhammad* (New Delhi, 1991).

Ahmed, Nisar, *The Fundamental Teachings of Quran and Hadith*, 2 vols (Karachi, 1969).

Alfahim, A.R.I., *The 200 Hadith: 200 Sayings and Doings of the Prophet Muhammad* (pbuh) (Makkah, 1990).

Azizullah, Muhammad (trans.), *Glimpses of the Hadith* (Maryland, 1972).

Doi, A.R., *Introduction to Hadith* (Lagos, 1970).

D'Oyen, Fatima M. and Chachi, Abdelkader, *In the Prophet's Garden: A Selection of Ahadith for the Young* (Markfield, UK, 2002).

Elias, A.H., *Learn a Hadith a Day* (Northmead, SA, 1996).

Halimah, A.M., *The Wisdom of the Prophet (pbuh)* (London, 2000).

Hasani, S.A.H., *Tahdhib al-Akhlaq: A Hadith Guide for personal and social conduct* (Leicester, 2003).

Hixon, Lex and Ferrahi, Fariha Ali (trans.), *101 Diamonds from the Tradition of the Glorious Messenger Muhammad (pbuh)* (New York, 2002).

Ibrahim, Ezzeddin, *Forty Hadith* (Chicago, 1982).

Kazi, Mazhar U., *A Treasury of Hadith and Sunnah* (Delhi, 1998).

Siddiqi, Abdul Hameed, *Selections from Hadith* (New Delhi, 1979).

Yusuf, Hamza (trans.), *The Content of Character: Ethical Sayings of the Prophet Muhammad*, collected by Al-Amin Ali Mazrui (England, 2005).

Classical Collections of the Prophet's Sayings

Abdur Rehman, Rafique, *The Translation of the Meanings of Jami' al-Tirmidhi*, 2 vols (Karachi, 2007).

Asad, Muhammad (trans.), *Sahih al-Bukhari: the early years of Islam* (Gibraltar, 1981).

Ansari, Mohammad Tufail (trans.), *Sunan Ibn Majah*, 5 vols (Delhi, n.d.)

Clarke, Abdassamad (trans.), *Imam Nawawi's Forty Hadith* (London, 1998).

DeLorenzo, Yusuf (trans.), *Imam Bukhari's Book of Muslim Morals and Manners* (Beirut, 1997).

Hamid, Abdul Ali (trans.) *Moral Teachings of Islam: Prophetic Traditions from Bukhari's* Al-Adab al-Mufrad (Oxford, 2003).

Hasan, Ahmad (trans.) *Sunan Abu Dawud: English translation with explanatory notes*, 3 vols (London, 1984).

Husain, S. Athar (trans.) *A Selection from Mishkat-ul-Masabeeh* (Lucknow, 1980).

Ibrahim, Ezzeddin and Johnson-Davies, Denys (trans.), *Al-Nawawi's Forty Hadith* (Safat, Kuwait, 1985).

Karim, Fazlur, *Al-Hadis: An English Translation and Commentary of Mishkat-ul-Masabih*, 4 vols (Lahore, 1979).

Khan, M. Muhsin (trans.), *Sahih al-Bukhari*, 9 vols (Ankara, 1976).

al-Khattab, Nasruddin (trans.), *Sunan al-Nasa'i*, 6 vols. (Riyadh, 2007).

Rahimuddin, Muhammad (trans.), *Imam Malik's Muwatta'* (Lahore, 1980).

Robson, James (trans.) *Mishkat al-Masabih: English translation with explanatory notes*, 2 vols (Lahore, 1981).

Siddiqi, Abdul Hamid (trans.) *Sahih Muslim*, 4 vols (Delhi, 1977).

Shad, Abdur Rehman (trans.) *Riyad as-Salihin* (Lahore, 1984).

Tarjumana, Aisha and Johnson, Yaqub (trans.) *Imam Malik's Al-Muwatta'* (Norwich, UK, 1982).

Critical Works and Commentaries on Hadith

Anees, M.A. and Athar, A., *Guide to Sira and Hadith Literature in Western Languages* (London, 1986).

Azami, Muhammad Mustafa, *Studies in Early Hadith Literature* (Burn Ridge, USA, 2001).

Dihlawi, Abdul Aziz, *The Garden of the Hadith Scholars* (London, 2007).

Ghaffar, Suhaib Hasan, *Criticism of Hadith among Muslims with reference to Sunan Ibn Majah* (Riyadh, 1987).

Al-Hanbali, Ibn Rajab, *The Compendium of Knowledge and Wisdom* (London, 2007).

Hoosen, Abdool Kader, *Imam Tirmidhi's contribution towards Hadith* (Newcastle, South Africa, 1990).

Kamali, Muhammad Hashim, *A Textbook of Hadith Studies* (Markfield, UK, 2005).

Nadwi, Muhammad Akram, *Al-Muhaddithat: The Women Scholars in Islam* (Oxford, 2007).

Nadwi, S. Abul Hasan Ali, *Role of Hadith in the promotion of Islamic climate and attitudes* (Lucknow, 1982).

Nadwi, Syed Sulaiman, *Human Rights and Obligations in the Light of the Quran and Hadith* (Karachi, 1996).

Nomani, M. Manzoor, *Meaning and Message of the Traditions*, 5 vols (Lucknow, 1989).

Siddiqi, Muhammad Zubayr, *Hadith Literature: Its Origin, Development and Special Features*, rev. ed. (Cambridge, 1993).

Daily Wisdom

Sayings of the Prophet Muhammad

God has sent me to profess and practise moral values and deeds. (SS)

O God! Purify my heart of hypocrisy, my actions of pretence, my tongue of lies, and my eyes of deception. For You know well the deception of the eye and all that is concealed in the heart. (KU)

Avoid suspicion, for suspicion is often baseless. Do not spy on each other. Do not probe into the affairs of others. Nor indulge in worldliness or jealousy. Do not bear grudges against each other. Nor betray anyone. Rather lead your lives as servants of God and live as brothers. (MK)

In both your private and public life you should always fear God. Piety should inform your conduct. Your good deeds will help in getting your sins forgiven. Treat people well. (A/T)

Anyone who has these three traits is definitely a hypocrite: (i) he tells a lie whenever he says something; (ii) he does not keep his word whenever he makes a promise; and (iii) he cheats when a trust is placed in his care. (B/M)

Follow the middle path. Taking up what is beyond your capacity will only bring shame upon you. (T)

I have little to do with this world. My worldly life is no more than the halting of a traveller, taking rest under the shade of a tree for a moment and then moving on. (A/T/I)

The Prophet ﷺ was never seen eating while reclining against a cushion. Nor did he let anyone walk behind him. (D/MSH)

Faith in God guides humanity to give up all that is vain and trivial. (A/MK)

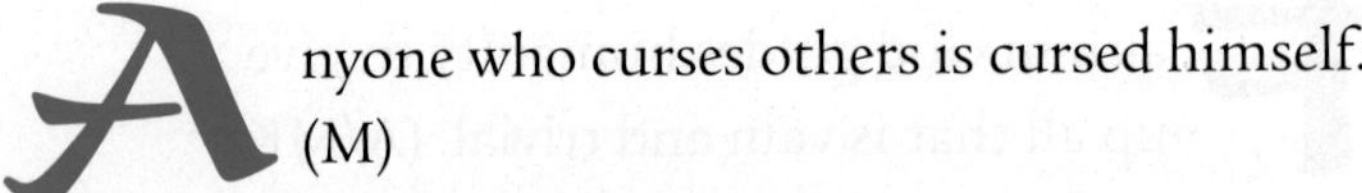

Anyone who curses others is cursed himself. (M)

A hypocrite will suffer most in the After-life. As he will be consigned to Hell and his entrails will be roasted, the inmates of Hell will gather around him and ask what had brought such a dreadful punishment upon him, for during his life he used to exhort people to do good and shun evil. In reply he will confess that notwithstanding his preaching, he himself did not practise the same. He committed the very sins he used to warn everyone else about. (B)

Anyone who loves God and His Messenger and who seeks to win their pleasure should (i) always speak the truth; (ii) justify the trust in which he is held; and (iii) be a good neighbour.

The Prophet ﷺ was informed about a woman who was known for her devotion to prayer, fasting and charity. However, she used to insult her neighbours with offensive comments. He dubbed her an inmate of Hell. On the other hand, he branded another woman a dweller of Paradise who was kind to her neighbours, although she did not perform any extra prayers. (A/BQ)

A widow's marriage was arranged by her father without her consent. She did not like her new husband. When she approached the Prophet ﷺ, he annulled her marriage. (B)

You should not make a marriage proposal, if another proposal is being considered. You should only go ahead if that proposal falls through. (B/M)

Wealth does not consist in abundant provision and plenty of goods. A truly rich person is content, enjoying peace of mind. (B)

Simple living is a sure sign of true faith. (D/M)

There is a cure for every disease. A medical remedy best suited to that disease cures one at God's command. (M)

Do not treat any good deed lightly. It is part of good manners to receive your brother or friend warmly. The same holds true for doing them a favour, no matter how small it might be. (T)

If you want plentiful sustenance and a long life, then you should maintain your family ties properly. (B/M)

If you seek wealth, while using fair means, to become financially independent, supporting your family and helping your neighbours, then you will be raised on the Day of Judgement with your face shining as brightly as the full moon. However, if you only seek worldly glory and amass wealth in order to make a show and to earn people's praise, then you will face God's wrath on the Day of Judgement. (BQ)

Do not pile up property or possessions lest you become desirous of this world. (T)

I fear the appearance of such eloquent orators in your midst whose speech will be marked by profundity and high morals yet their deeds will reek of evil and wickedness. (BQ/MSH)

Do not be like those who are good only to those who are kind to them. Do not wrong him who wrongs you. You should be kind even to those hostile towards you. You should not follow them in their wrongdoing. (MSH)

Charity does not decrease one's wealth. Nor does humility lower one's prestige. If one acts humbly for God's sake, then God will certainly raise one's rank. (M)

If you wrong or overburden your allies or usurp what rightfully belongs to them, I will fight their case against yours on the Day of Judgement. (D)

He who makes a false claim on something that is not his is not a believer. Such dishonesty will land him in Hell. (M)

Taking back a gift is as odious as a dog licking its own vomit. (B/MSH)

If you are in doubt about the propriety of an act, do not do it. Rather, you should only do what you know to be good. The truth blesses you with peace of mind while falsehood torments you with uneasiness and tension. (T/N)

The one who has even an iota of pride in his heart cannot enter Paradise. By the same token, the one who has a grain of faith will not be hurled into Hell. (M)

Your neighbours are the best judges of your conduct. If they speak highly of you, you are blessed with good morals and manners. If they speak ill of you, it is a pointer to your bad conduct. (I/MSH)

The community does not attain to piety if it does not take good care of the weak and the poor. (MSH)

The one who usurps someone's property, even if it be a twig, by taking a false oath [of ownership], cannot enter Paradise. God has ordained Hell for him. (M)

A believer perceives his misdeeds as a rock that is about to crush him whereas a wicked person dismisses his sins like shooing a fly away. (B)

Pay charity (*Zakah*) on your wealth, for it is truly a purifier that cleanses you. Be kind to your relatives and fulfil the rights of the poor, neighbours and beggars. (M)

The best one among you is he who is kind to his wife and children. I am an example in this. (M)

The one who harms others will be punished by God. The one who is hostile towards others, God will afflict him with hardship. (T)

The Prophet ﷺ asked those sitting beside him, "Do you think there would be any impurity or dirt on the body of someone who bathes five times a day in a river flowing in front of his house?" When they emphatically ruled it out, he explained, "My parable alludes to the five obligatory prayers a day. God overlooks one's sins as reward for his offering the five daily prayers regularly." (B)

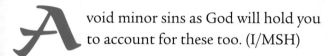

Avoid minor sins as God will hold you to account for these too. (I/MSH)

When one visits a sick person, he is enveloped by God's mercy. As long as he stays with the sick, he is rewarded with God's mercy. (MSH)

Prayer is the comfort of my eyes. (B/M)

A perfect believer is he who is of excellent character. The best ones among you are those who treat their wives well. (B)

Treat your children with kindness and affection. Take care of their moral upbringing. (I)

A labourer once passed by the Prophet ﷺ who was seated with his Companions. Those present commented that if his toil had been in God's cause, it would have been better for him. The Prophet ﷺ, however, corrected them, saying: "If his efforts are geared towards supporting his children, he is still working in God's cause. The same holds true if his objective is to provide sustenance for his parents. Even if his striving aims at earning some income that would save him from begging from others, then he is working in God's way. It is only if his motive is to make a show of his wealth, then he is following in Satan's footsteps." (B)

When one dies, one's record of deeds is sealed. However, for the following three deeds, one continues to earn God's reward, even after one's death:
(i) an endowment for some charitable work; (ii) leaving behind such scholarly works that may benefit subsequent generations; and (iii) virtuous children who pray for their parents. (KU)

DAY 46

He who acts kindly towards those relatives who are good to him does not do real justice to the ties of kinship; rather, he who discharges this obligation perfectly maintains ties of kinship even with those who sever relations with him. (B)

A dutiful, loving son who looks at his parents with love and kindness will earn a reward equal to performing the Hajj (Pilgrimage) for each loving glance of his. Even if he casts such a glance one hundred times a day, he would be credited with the same reward each time. Almighty God's treasure is never diminished by such generous and lavish rewards. (BQ)

A Muslim who plants a tree or farms the land is rewarded for giving in charity, as humans and other creatures eat of his produce, even if he does not give it willingly to them. (M/A)

On being asked to name the best charitable act, the Prophet ﷺ replied, "The charity given to your poor relative who is hostile to you stands out as the best kind of charity." (TT)

No one can enter Paradise by dint of his deeds alone. May God envelop us in His mercy and affection. Follow the way of faith steadfastly. Do not wish for death. For if you are good, you had better repent for as long as you live for that would be pleasing to God. (B)

Whenever some good news reached the Prophet ﷺ, he used to fall down in prostration, giving thanks to God. (B)

od loves the believer who works hard to earn his bread. (TB)

If you grant relief to the borrower, God will be lenient with you on the Day of Recompense. (M/MSH)

If one promotes someone's interests and accepts a gift in return, he commits a sinister evil act. (D)

One may devote one's whole life to acts of worship and in strict obedience to God yet one may end up in Hell for having denied one's heirs their due, by leaving behind an unfair bequest. (T/D)

A woman of the influential tribe of Makhzum committed theft. Her tribesmen asked Usama, who was very close to the Prophet ﷺ, to say some kind words about her so that she might be spared the punishment prescribed by Islamic law. As he recommended her case, the Prophet ﷺ chided him for perverting the course of justice. Immediately he summoned a public meeting in which he delivered the following address, "O people! Earlier communities faced Divine punishment as they used to enforce the penal code only on the weak and the poor while the powerful among them got away with their crimes. By God, even if my daughter, Fatima, were to commit theft, I would impose on her the punishment ordained by Islamic law." (B/M)

The one who blindly supports an unjust act of his family, tribe or community follows the path of self-destruction. (D)

Judges are of three kinds: (i) those who decide cases honestly will have Paradise as their abode; (ii) those who decide cases dishonestly will end up in Hell; and (iii) those who decide cases frivolously, without ascertaining the truth, will also be consigned to Hell. (D/I)

Punish alike those who are your kin and those who are not. Do not be cowed by anyone's criticism in enforcing justice in accordance with God's commands. (I/MSH)

Do not indulge in backbiting. Nor should you pry into or publicize the failings of others. Whoever is guilty of it will be treated likewise by God – and he is bound is to be disgraced publicly. (D)

Those of you who have excellent conduct will enjoy my company, but those with ill-manners and sharp, reproaching tongues will be kept away from me. (BQ/MSH)

On retiring to bed, say: "O God! I live and die in Your name." On getting up: "All praise and thanks be to God Who revived me. To Him is the return when we will be resurrected after death." (M)

O Lord! Bless me with the best of conduct. You alone can guide me in this. Help me shed all that is unworthy in my conduct, for only You can enable me to do so. (M)

O God! Increase my sustenance in my old age and at the end of my life. (H)

Once the Prophet ﷺ asked his Companions: "Who do you think is a poor person?" They replied: "The one who does not have money or possessions." He clarified, however, that: "The poor one among my community is he whose record of deeds on the Day of Judgement would, no doubt, include his prayers, fasting and payment of charity (*Zakah*). However, his record will also list his misdeeds such as abusing and slandering others, his usurping the belongings of others, and his striking or killing people. In recompense, his good deeds will be credited to his victims, so he will not get any reward for his good acts. If this does not settle his tally, then even the sins committed by his victims will be transferred to his account, which will lead to him being hurled into Hell. This is the person who is really poor." (M)

True wealth does not consist in possessing abundant resources, but in having a contented heart. (B)

Anyone who knowingly connives with an unjust oppressor stands outside the fold of faith. (MSH)

Anyone who shares food with his servants, rides a donkey in the marketplace, and milks his goat possesses excellent conduct, free from the blemishes of pride and arrogance. (M)

Many people will be admitted to Paradise on account of their piety and excellent morals and manners. By the same token, many will be consigned to Hell for not having protected their tongues and their private parts. (T)

The following four traits make up excellent character: (i) trustworthiness; (ii) truthfulness; (iii) politeness; and (iv) living on lawful earnings. (T)

DAY 71

Arousing jealousy in others is only allowed in two circumstances: (i) he who is blessed by God with wealth and spends it lavishly on the cause of truth; and (ii) he who is favoured by God with wisdom, decides cases prudently and instructs people in wisdom. (B/A)

The one who is not kind-hearted and considerate is unable to perform many good acts. (M)

He is not a liar who tells white lies in order to bring peace between two quarrelling parties and conveys to them such a message that they may draw close to each other. (B/M)

A generous person draws near to God, gets closer to Paradise, and becomes distant from Hell. In contrast, a miser is far removed from God and Paradise and falls headlong into Hell. God loves a generous person, who may not be very well-versed in religious knowledge, more than that miser who is engaged in acts of worship. (T)

Two people who were fasting offered prayer behind the Prophet ﷺ. On noting that they were backbiting, the Prophet ﷺ asked them to repeat their prayer and to observe their fast again the next day as expiation for their backbiting. (BQ)

He whose neighbours are not safe from his mischief and evil will not be admitted to Paradise. (M)

Anyone who has no shame before people has no shame before God. (TB)

One is rewarded for helping a needy person who is not a relative. However, one gets a double reward for helping a needy relative: one reward for charity and another for fulfilling obligations towards the ties of kinship. (N/T)

Bringing peace between hostile parties is a more blessed act than engaging in prayers, fasting or charity. By the same token, causing discord in society is something horribly destructive. (D)

Of all that God has bestowed upon humanity, the most invaluable is good character and conduct. (BQ)

The dearest to me among my Companions are those who have good conduct. (B)

The archangel Gabriel (who brought divine revelation) impressed upon me so much the command to treat neighbours well that I thought neighbours would also get a share in inheritance. (B)

A true believer embodies overflowing love and affection. The one who does not love others is devoid of any virtue. He is detested by everyone. (A/BQ)

The one who is unmerciful will not be shown mercy by God. (M)

If one bears patiently with his loss and suffering in order to please God, he will be admitted to Paradise. (I)

God being the Most Compassionate is merciful towards those who show kindness. Be kind to your fellow human beings, and your Lord will shower mercy upon you. (D/T)

You should not ask anyone to give up his seat for you. Rather you should make room for each other. (B/M)

On coming to know of someone's misdeed, the Prophet ﷺ would not name the culprit in his sermonizing. Rather, he would warn people against the evil of that misdeed in general terms. (D)

DAY 89

Be on your guard against the corroding vice of jealousy. It wipes out one's good deeds as rapidly as fire destroys wood. (D)

The one who takes the lead in greeting others comes closer to God. (A/T)

If you lead the prayer, remember the old and the weak of your congregation standing behind you. Therefore, do not prolong the prayer. However, when praying alone, you may prolong your prayer as much as you like. (B/M)

Do not rejoice at some calamity befalling another, for God might relieve him and afflict you with the same. (T)

God loves His self-respecting servant who, while poor, avoids begging from others. (I)

Strive to earn your bread lawfully: it is one of your most important duties. (BQ)

On being asked how many times one should pardon his servant, the Prophet ﷺ replied, "Overlook his lapses seventy times a day." (T)

Once, when addressing his followers, the Prophet ﷺ cautioned them, “I am a human being like you. You refer your disputes to me for judgment. The more articulate among you may persuade me to decide the case in his favour. If I were ever to do so, then do not go by my judgement, for what I might have awarded to you on the basis of your false testimony would take you straight to Hell.” (B/M)

The true believer does not harm anyone with his tongue or by his hand. (B)

As your servant prepares food for you, he does a painstaking, toilsome job. You are obliged to seat him beside you when you eat. (M/MSH)

All the believers constitute a single fraternity. They do not betray, cheat or wrong one another. Rather, each believer holds up a mirror to the others to alert them to their lapses. (T/ MSH)

Whereas God may defer punishment for one's other sins until the Day of Recompense, the one guilty of denying his parents their due and disobeying them is punished in this world in addition to the punishment that will be inflicted upon him in the Hereafter. (BQ)

The one who lusts after name and fame will be disgraced by God on the Day of Judgement. (D/MSH)

'A'ishah, the Prophet's wife, is on record as saying that the Prophet ﷺ used to assist her with domestic chores. (B)

The wife whose husband is content with her until his death will enter Paradise. (N)

He is not a believer who has a square meal while his neighbour starves. (I)

Beware! I give you a strong warning regarding your obligations towards the weak, and especially the rights of orphans and women. (RS)

Blessed is the wedding that does not entail any financial burden. (BQ)

If you repose trust in God in a befitting manner, He will sustain you in the same manner as He feeds the birds. Birds leave their nests at dawn on empty stomachs and return at dusk with their bellies full. (T/MSH)

The one who gets something from someone should return the favour, if he can afford it. The one unable to do so should, at least, praise and thank his benefactor. This amounts to repaying the favour done to him. On the other hand, the one who refuses to acknowledge the favour done to him is an ungrateful wretch. (T/D)

Such are the chosen servants of God that one instinctively remembers God on meeting them. And the worst of His servants are those who sow discord between people and falsely implicate the innocent. (A/BQ)

You are not superior to any black or white person. You may excel others only by virtue of your piety. (A)

When a sinner turns to God in repentance, it pleases Him as much as a traveller in a desert is delighted to find his lost camel. (B/M)

O my Lord! I seek from You the ability to ask of You what is best for me: the best supplication, comprehensive success, abiding reward, and a worthy life and death. Keep me steadfast. Weigh down the scale of my good deeds. Strengthen my faith. Raise my rank. Accept my prayers. I ask of You the highest rank in Paradise. (H)

You cannot be a true believer unless you love for your brother or your neighbour what you love for yourself. (M)

Someone asked the Prophet ﷺ whether he should tie his camel or let it loose, entrusting it to God's care. He directed him to tie it securely first and then entrust it to God's protection. (T)

Of all the worldly bounties, the most valuable one is a good wife. (M/N)

A worker's wages represent the best of income, provided that he does his job sincerely and diligently. (A)

T the one who deprives his heir of his share in inheritance will be denied any share in Paradise. (I)

God forgives every sin of the martyr except for the outstanding loan that he had taken from someone. (M)

If you get rid of an evil in your society, God will spare you. The same holds true for him who can only protest against it, if it is beyond his capacity to remove it. Even he who resents it in his heart of hearts will not be taken to task by God if he was not in a position to remove or denounce it. However, the mere detesting of an evil represents the weakest degree of faith. (N)

If one intends to do a wrong act, God directs the angels not to record it until he actually does it. Once he commits it, only a single evil act is recorded against him. Conversely, if one intends to do a good deed, yet fails to do so, it is credited to him as a good act. If he actually performs a good act, he gets a tenfold reward. (M)

If three of you are travelling together, you should take one of you as a leader to oversee arrangements. (D)

Make the most of these while you still have them: (i) youth before becoming aged; (ii) prosperity before affliction with adversity; (iii) leisure before being overwhelmed with work; (iv) good health before falling ill; and (v) life before breathing your last. (T)

God commands that humanity's conduct be characterized by the following traits: (i) fearing God in private and public; (ii) adhering to justice whether the parties concerned are friendly or hostile; (iii) following the middle path in both prosperity and adversity; (iv) maintaining ties of kinship with even those relatives who sever their ties and misbehave; (v) kindness towards even those who act unjustly, failing to give their due; (vi) forgiving those who offend and oppress others; (vii) reflecting on the Divine signs around us and on one's relationship with God in terms of taking stock of one's conduct; (viii) remembering God constantly by way of saying and doing what God has commanded; and (ix) drawing lessons from everything and enjoining people to do good. (R)

On coming to know that one of his Companions, 'Uthman ibn Mazun, had turned into an extreme ascetic, renounced his family life and was solely engaged day and night in acts of worship, the Prophet ﷺ sent for him and asked him to follow his way, saying: "Look! I sleep for a few hours at night and offer the early morning Prayer as well. I fast but not every day. I marry women and maintain my relations with them. You should fear God and not neglect the obligations that you owe to your family, your body and your guests. Your children have rights over you. Your body and your guests have rights over you too. Fast but eat as well. Pray but also sleep at night." (D)

If you fail to defend a fellow Muslim whose honour is under attack, despite an ability to do so, you will be punished by God in this life and the Next. (SS)

Someone who asks people attending to him to keep standing and enjoys doing so reserves a place for himself in Hell. (T/D)

O people! Seek God's forgiveness. I turn to Him in repentance one hundred times a day. (M)

Every human being is liable to commit sins. However, the best is he who repents of his sins. (T/I)

The one who constantly seeks God's forgiveness is shown a way out. God helps him to surmount every hardship and relieves him from every sorrow and worry. He provides him with sustenance from unexpected quarters. (A/D/I)

After the death of your father, you should maintain social ties with his friends. This constitutes a good act and a courtesy on your part. (M)

When a girl appeared before the Prophet ﷺ, he told her, "When a girl comes of age, she should keep her body covered. You may, however, keep your face and hands uncovered." (M)

There are some poetic couplets that abound with wisdom. (B/M)

Labid [an Arab poet of the Prophet's day] articulated a profound truth in his couplet, "Beware! Everyone other than God is ephemeral and mortal." (B/M)

What you eat, and what you provide in food for your wife, your children and your servants, constitutes an act of charity. (AM)

You may serve and please your parents, even after their death, by (i) praying for their forgiveness and deliverance; (ii) honouring the commitments made by them; (iii) treating their friends well; and (iv) maintaining their ties of kinship. (AM)

It is an obligation like any other religious duty to strive to earn a lawful income. (MSH)

Once someone came to the Prophet ﷺ, crying profusely over a major sin he had committed, and asked how he should atone for it. The Prophet ﷺ asked whether his parents were alive. When he said no, the Prophet ﷺ directed him to serve and take good care of his maternal aunt. (T)

The best thing that parents can give their children is excellent moral upbringing and training. (MSH)

It is binding upon you to obey your ruler, whether you like his commands or not. You are not, however, obliged to follow him if he asks you to defy any of the Divine commandments. (MSH)

A ruler who does not take good care of his subjects will be dragged by his face and hurled into Hell on the Day of Judgement. (TB)

Murder will be the first matter taken up on the Day of Reckoning. (B/M)

DAY 142

Everyone will have to answer five questions on the Day of Judgement:

(i) How did you lead your life?

(ii) How far did you act on the religious knowledge that you gained?

(iii) How did you earn your wealth?

(iv) How did you spend your wealth?

(v) What did you busy your life with?

(T)

By God, if you were to know in full the reality of God's wrath and the dreadful scenes of the Day of Judgment, which are in my [the Prophet's] knowledge, you would cry profusely and cease laughing. (B)

The Prophet ﷺ defined backbiting thus, "Speaking of someone is such terms as might offend him." Someone inquired as to whether mentioning someone's failings amounted to backbiting. The Prophet ﷺ affirmed, "This is what backbiting is. Otherwise, if you ascribe to him a failing that he does not have, it constitutes slander, which is a more heinous sin than backbiting." (M)

An honest, trustworthy businessman will enjoy the privileged company of God's Messengers, the truthful ones and the martyrs in the Next Life. (T)

He who violates the codes of morality and justice to help someone unlawfully will end up as an utter loser in the Next Life. In so doing, he courts his own loss in the Hereafter. (MSH)

On observing someone using a lot of water for ablution, the Prophet ﷺ censured him. He asked him not to waste a drop of water even when he is beside a river. (A/MSH)

The following evils will become rampant before the end of the world: (i) only the elite will be greeted while the commoners will be contemptuously neglected; (ii) the craze for amassing wealth and a higher standard of living will be such that wives would be full-time business partners with their husbands; (iii) ties of kinship will be disregarded altogether; (iv) an explosion in knowledge that is without benefit; and (v) false testimony will be fairly common, as no one will come forward to testify to the truth. (AM)

O my Lord! I am weak and helpless. Grant me the strength to do all that pleases You. Help me to do good eagerly. Make faith my goal. I am humble and disgraced, so grant me honour and glory. I am needy, so bless me with sustenance. (H)

Leave what makes you doubt for what does not. (T)

On being asked to name the best means of income, the Prophet ﷺ answered, "Manual work and fair trading." (MSH)

While selling your goods, do not take recourse to false, misleading oaths. This might boost your business for a while, but, in the long run, you would not attain prosperity. (M)

When you sneeze, you should say, "Praise be to God." Those around you should respond by saying, "May God have mercy on you." In return, that person should offer this supplication, "May God grant you guidance and improve your affairs." (B)

On visiting the sick, say: "O Lord! Remove his or her suffering. You alone can grant a cure. Bestow such a cure as may eliminate his or her disease altogether." (M)

On the Day of Judgement, the earth will testify to all the acts of every man and woman, presenting an accurate record of every deed. (TA)

On visiting the sick say, "O Lord of men! Relieve him of his pain and suffering. Grant him full recovery, free from every disease. Only You can provide a cure. No one other than You can cure him." (M)

O Lord! Grant us increase and do not afflict us with loss. Exalt us and do not abase us. Bestow bounties upon us and do not deprive us. (B/M)

O God! We seek from You the ways and means to attain forgiveness, deliverance and protection from all sins. We seek from You an abundance of good, entry into Paradise and protection from Hellfire. (KU)

O God! Bless me with patience and gratitude. Humble me in my own eyes while exalting me in the eyes of others. (KU)

O God! Bless our country with abundance, prosperity and peace. Do not deprive me of the fruits of what You have granted me. Do not test me with what you have not given me. (KU)

O God! You have created me in the best of moulds. Make my conduct equally excellent. Remove from my heart all ill-feeling and protect me until my death from the lures of those who would misguide me. (A)

What to say when leaving home, "In the name of God I depart, placing my trust in God. There is no power or strength except in God." (M)

They will be denied God's mercy who do not show kindness to others. (B/M)

Your deliverance or perdition rely upon the following: (i) fear of God in both your private and public lives; (ii) standing by the truth whether it suits or harms your interests; (iii) moderation in both poverty and prosperity; (iv) avoiding addiction to base desires; (v) avoiding greed and lust; and (vi) avoiding self-centredness. (BQ)

The believers are like a house in which every brick is inseparably joined with every other. They should help one another when in distress. (MSH)

A true believer is one who practises what he preaches. Moreover, he should not cause his neighbour any problems. (TT)

When joining a gathering one should not disturb those already seated. And they should cheerfully make room for the newcomer. (A)

Modesty is part of true faith and it encourages goodness. (M)

Ponder contentment carefully, for it is a bounty without measure. (TB)

The Prophet ﷺ recounted the following incident: "Once, as a traveller quenched his thirst at a well, he saw a dog panting out of thirst. He offered water in his moccasin to the dog. God appreciated this good deed of his so much that He granted him deliverance." Those present asked in astonishment whether they would get any reward for kindness to animals. He affirmed it strongly, adding that there is Divine reward for showing kindness to any living being. (B/M)

If anyone afflicted with distress, be it physical or financial, does not complain, then God will grant him Paradise. (TB)

The expiation for backbiting is that the one guilty of it should pray earnestly to God that his victim be blessed with God's mercy. (JS)

Only conduct will carry weight on a believer's scale on the Day of Judgement. (D/T)

Islam does not allow monasticism. (D)

Cursed be the one who mutilates animals. (B)

An orphan's guardian and I (the Prophet ﷺ) will be as close to each other in Paradise as are my two fingers. (M)

At the time of creating the universe, God proclaimed: "My mercy far exceeds My anger." (B/M/T)

You will be deemed a liar if you report whatever you hear without verification. (M/MSH)

Someone requested the Prophet ﷺ to give him some advice. He advised him: "Do not lose your temper." When he sought another piece of advice, the Prophet ﷺ repeated the same: "Do not lose your temper." (B)

The worst person is he whom people avoid because of his bad manners. God will deal harshly with him on the Day of Judgement. (D)

The Prophet ﷺ passed by a group of men, including Muslims, Jews and idolaters, and he greeted all of them with the customary Islamic greeting, "Peace and blessings be upon you". (B/M)

Do not vie with those who are better off than you. It will help you appreciate all the more what God has given you. (M)

A Muslim owes the following obligations to his fellow Muslims: (i) he should call on them when they fall ill; (ii) he should attend their funerals; (iii) he should pay them social visits; (iv) he should greet them on meeting them; (v) he should respond to their sneezing by saying "May God have mercy on you"; and (vi) he should act sincerely towards them. (N)

od is Beautiful and He loves beauty. (M)

When a baby girl is born to a family, God deputes angels to proclaim, "O members of this family! Blessings be upon you." Then they take the infant girl under their wings, stroke her hair and say, "Here is a weak, helpless being. The one who brings her up will enjoy God's support until the Last Day." (TB)

Your best charity is the one given to those dependent upon you. (D/MSH)

Gentleness is never part of anything without improving it, nor is it taken away from anything without debasing it. (BQ)

Remember God and He will remember you. Keep invoking God and you will find Him with you. Seek whatever you need only from Him. Whenever you are in distress, call only on Him for aid. Even if all humanity came together to help you, they could not do so: you would only get what God has ordained for you. Likewise, if all of them intend to harm you, they cannot do so, excepting what God has already decreed for you. (MSH)

Among the believers the perfect one is he who excels most in good character and conduct. The best one among you is he who is kind to the women under his care. (T)

A Muslim who feeds a hungry Muslim will be served with the food of Paradise by God on the Day of Judgment.
A Muslim who offers water to a thirsty Muslim will be provided with an excellent sealed drink on the Day of Judgment.
A Muslim who clothes a poor Muslim will be dressed in the garments of Paradise on the Day of Judgement. (T)

Do not delay the following: (i) pray as soon as it is time for prayer; (ii) bury your dead as soon as the coffin is ready; and (iii) marry your daughter as soon as you find a suitable match for her. (T)

One blessed with true faith cannot fall prey to greed and miserliness. These vices are incompatible with true faith. (N)

A true believer is he who neither vilifies nor curses anyone, nor does he utter obscene or abusive words. (T)

Disregard the person who praises you to your face. (M)

Anyone who does not reveal the faults of others will enjoy God's protection on the Day of Judgement. In reward, God will overlook his faults. (M)

If you take advice from others before taking an important step, you will not regret your decision later. Likewise, if you always follow the middle path, marked by moderation and prudence, you will not end up a pauper. (TB)

That wife can never enter Paradise who seeks separation from her husband without an urgent and valid reason. (A/T)

Condemned is he who takes a child away from its mother. (BQ)

The beauty of Islam lies in minding one's own business. (T)

You are free to eat, drink and dress as it pleases you, so long as you do not betray pride and refrain from extravagance. (B)

You are much influenced by the company you keep. Before you befriend someone, assess his convictions and character. (A/MSH)

Circumspection is from God and hastiness is from the devil. (BQ)

The one who believes in God and the Day of Judgement should either speak well or observe silence. (B/M)

Virtue consists in your good conduct and evil is that deed which pricks your conscience or that you would not like others to know about. (M)

He is not a believer whose neighbour is unsafe from his mischief and wrongdoing. (M)

A die-hard hypocrite is one who always (i) betrays the trust reposed in him; (ii) resorts to telling lies; (iii) fails to keep his word; and (iv) uses filthy, abusive language in a quarrel. Beware! If you have even one of the above traits, then you will be reckoned as a hypocrite. (MSH)

On being blessed with a child, parents should first give him a good name and ensure his moral upbringing. As he comes of age, they should arrange for his marriage. Otherwise, they will be accountable, if he indulges in pre-marital sex. (BQ)

If your parents die and you were unable to serve them properly, all is not lost. You should consistently seek God's forgiveness for your deceased parents. On the Day of Judgment you will be reckoned as their devoted, obedient child. (BQ)

The father who neither buries his daughter alive [as the pagan Arabs did] nor degrades her and who does not prefer her over his son will be admitted to Paradise. (D)

Spend your wealth! Do not keep counting it as God will give to you in unrestricted measure, so do not be miserly. Otherwise, God will not give to you abundantly, so give as much as you can. (B/M)

The human heart, like iron, is liable to rust. The remembrance of death and recitation of the Qur'an protects the heart from getting tarnished. (MSH)

I say this with all the force at my command that usurping the rights of these two disadvantaged parts of society - orphans and women - is a major sin. (N)

A trader who does not resort to hoarding earns God's mercy whereas the one guilty of it is accursed. (I)

The best worshipper is he who looks forward to excellent recompense from his Lord. (A/D)

God offered to me abundant wealth: valleys of Makkah overflowing with gold were presented before me. However, I submitted to Him, "I do not seek wealth. Rather, I prefer to eat one day and to sleep on an empty stomach the next. For, on feeling hungry, I would turn more fervently to You and invoke You humbly. And, when blessed with food, I would grow more grateful to You." (A/T)

God has provided a cure for every disease. (B)

God blesses business partners so long as they are honest and sincere with each other. However, if one of them starts cheating the other, then God withdraws His blessings from them. (D)

That ruler who causes hardship to the public will be harshly punished by God. On the other hand, the ruler who is kind and affectionate to his subjects will be blessed with God's mercy in the Hereafter. (M)

The wisest among you is he who is ever-conscious of death and prepares himself for it. He gains the best of both the worlds: he is honoured in life and will be warmly received in the Hereafter. (TB)

On the Day of Judgement one will enjoy shade and comfort as a reward for one's charitable deeds. (A)

God does not look at your faces or your riches, but only at your deeds and your innermost feelings. (M)

O God! I seek refuge in You from knowledge which is not beneficial, from the supplication that goes unanswered, from the heart that does not fear You, and from the self that is never contented. (I)

While all other human beings will roast in the scorching heat of the Day of Judgement, the following will be seated beneath God's Throne, enjoying shade and comfort: (i) the fair and just ruler; (ii) the youth who spent his time in worship; (iii) the one who often went to the mosque to pray; (iv) one who loved to meet others only for God's sake; (v) the one who was seduced by a woman of beauty and rank yet who spurned her out of the fear of God; (vi) the one who gave secretly in charity, without bringing it to anyone's knowledge; and (vii) the one who remembered God in private and cried out in fear of God. (B)

O God! I seek from You beneficial knowledge. (BQ)

O God! Forgive my sins, both inadvertent and deliberate. (B)

O God! Help me lead life humbly and cause me to die in a state of humility. Include me among those who are humble. (KA)

O God! Make me one of those who are pleased with doing something good and who seek Your forgiveness as soon as they do something wrong. (I)

What should we say when we travel by car, bus or other means of transport: Glory be to the One Who subjected this (car, plane, etc.) to our needs, otherwise, we would not have been able to accomplish it on our own. And we will surely return to our Lord in the end.
(Qur'an)

What should we say when we study:
O Lord! Increase me in knowledge.
(Qur'an)

My Lord! Forgive me and my parents and all the believers on the Day of Judgement. (Qur'an)

O my Lord! I seek from You the strength and ability to do good, to shun sin and to help the poor. May You grant me deliverance and have mercy on me. Make me die before You test me. I seek from You the strength and ability to love You and him who loves You and to prefer such acts that may draw me closer to You. (H)

Y ou are not better than any black or white person. If you are pious, it is this alone that makes you better than others. (A)

God is All Merciful and He showers compassion and mercy upon everyone. He gives abundantly to those who are kind-hearted, but not to those who are stern and unrelenting. (M)

Three traits characterize a believer's conduct: (i) even when in a fit of anger, he does not resort to falsehood; (ii) even when he is elated, he does not transgress the bounds of truth; and (iii) when he enjoys power, he does not deny people their due. (MSH)

On being asked whether a desire for good clothes betrays an inclination towards pride, the Prophet ﷺ replied, "God being the All-Radiant appreciates beauty. Pride, however, consists in looking down upon others and in opposing the truth." (M/MSH)

Anyone asked for advice should realize the importance of the trust being placed in him. (D)

It is not becoming of a believer to go to bed after having a full meal while his neighbour may have nothing to eat. (MSH)

O God! Let not a wicked person do me a favour that I may have to repay in this world or in the Next One. (KU)

The perfection of reason consists of taking steps with far-reaching results, piety in shunning sins, and excellent conduct in promoting noble virtues. (B/M)

The time spent on visiting the sick is credited to one's account as time given over to visiting the gardens of Paradise. (M)

There will come a time when a killer will not know why he killed someone and his victim will have no idea why he was killed. (M)

It does not befit a believer to curse (or insult) anyone. (T)

The best Muslim home is the one that houses an orphan who is looked after properly. The worst is one where the orphan is maltreated. (I/A)

Two of you should not whisper to each other in the presence of a third, for it would offend him. (M)

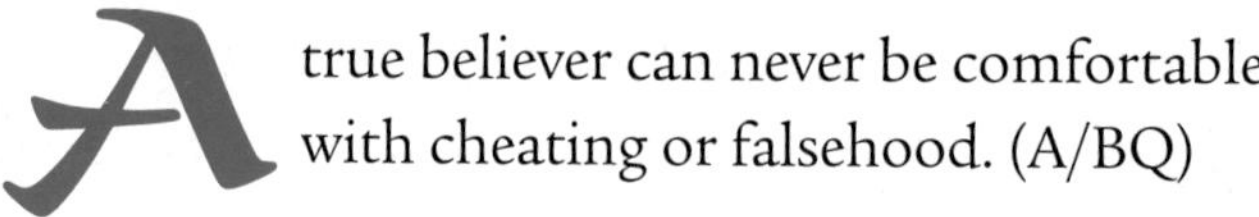

A true believer can never be comfortable with cheating or falsehood. (A/BQ)

Return even the needle and thread that you may have borrowed from someone. Your breach of trusts will bring disgrace to you on the Day of Judgement. (N/MSH)

Those who dispensed justice fairly will be seated on pulpits of light to the right of God. They will be lavishly rewarded for having acted with justice even in cases involving their family and relatives. (M)

DAY 248

He who wants to be fully protected from Hell and is keen to enter Paradise should breathe his last in a state of faith, believing in God and the Day of Judgement. He should behave with people in the same good manner that he wants them to treat him. (M)

The one engaged in remembering God is truly alive. By contrast, the one who disregards his Lord is like a corpse. (B/M)

The one who is neither affectionate towards the young nor respectful to the elderly, who neither enjoins the good nor forbids evil, is not one of us. (T)

The one who brings up three daughters, instructs them well in morals and manners, gets them married and treats them well will get a place in Paradise. (D)

Eat, drink, dress well and give in charity so long as it does not border on extravagance or showing off. (A/N)

If one gives some money in charity out of his unlawful earnings, God neither accepts nor blesses such income. The one guilty of getting money unlawfully is destined for Hell. (A)

The one who hoards grain is a sinner. (M/MSH)

A true worshipper believes in the essential goodness of others. (A/MSH)

Generally men select their prospective wives on the following criteria: her wealth, the social status of her family and her beauty. You should, however, only choose a marriage partner who is devout, giving priority only to her religiosity. (B)

ll creatures are part of God's family. God loves him most who is kind to His creatures. (MSH)

It is not lawful for a trader to sell an item, without pointing to its defects, if it has any. If he knows it to be defective, he is obliged to bring it to the customer's notice. (I)

A ruler who does not protect the interests of my community in the same way as he takes care of his own family will be denied entry into Paradise. (TB)

On the Day of Judgement God will instruct the angels to keep away from Hell all those who had ever remembered or feared Him in this world. (T/BQ)

O God! I earnestly seek from You beneficial knowledge, deeds acceptable to You, and lawful, wholesome sustenance. (I/A)

O God! You cause the hearts to incline towards something, so incline our hearts towards obeying You. (M)

When a believer makes a supplication to God, it is answered in one of three ways: it is fulfilled in this life, or recompensed in the next, or averts some calamity. (A)

Of all the permitted acts, divorce is the most detestable one in the sight of God. (D)

One's wealth does not decrease if one gives it in God's way. When one gives money in charity, it reaches God even before it is taken by its recipient. (TB)

DAY 266

Anas, who served the Prophet ﷺ for ten years, recounts, "I was a young boy when I became his servant. At times, I did not follow his instructions properly. However, during all those ten years he never rebuked me, nor did he ever grill me about my acts of forgetfulness or carelessness." (D)

When visiting a sick person the Prophet ﷺ used to comfort him: "Do not worry. This will, God willing, compensate for your acts of commission and omission." (B)

Exchange gifts with one another: it puts an end to any ill feeling in your hearts. (T)

If you defend the honour of your brother in his absence, by refuting a baseless charge against him, God will most certainly protect you from the punishment of Hellfire. (BQ)

Anyone who meets the need of a fellow Muslim pleases me. And anyone who pleases me is rewarded by God with Paradise. (BQ)

Do not be eager to encounter your enemy. Rather, seek God's safety and protection. However, once war is declared, be steadfast and consistent in fighting against the enemy. (B/M)

You must secure permission before entering the houses of even your own children, parents, brothers or sisters. (AM)

On being asked what one should dread most, the Prophet ﷺ pointed to the tongue, asserting that one should be very careful about what one says lest sins be incurred. (T)

The one who usurps someone's belongings by taking a false oath will appear as a leper before God on the Day of Judgment. (D)

He is a true believer who feels gratified on doing something good and is overcome with sorrow and remorse on doing anything evil. (H)

The first directive in the morning from the Prophet's Companions to their families was to feed the orphans and to take good care of them. (KU)

O Quraysh [my tribesmen]! Take steps to protect yourselves from Hellfire. I cannot release you from God's grip. O [my] family members of 'Abd al-Manaf! I cannot avert Divine punishment from you. O 'Abbas [my uncle]! I cannot be of any help to you on the Day of Judgement. O Safiya [my aunt]! I cannot delay Divine punishment for you even for a second. O my daughter, Fatima! I can give you as much of my wealth as I like. However, I cannot keep Divine punishment away from you. So all of you should strive for your deliverance. Your faith and good deeds alone will help you in the Afterlife. (B/M)

On being asked to curse the polytheists persecuting him, the Prophet ﷺ declared, "I have not been sent down in order to curse people. Rather, I have come as a mercy unto the world." (M)

Some people approached the Prophet ﷺ, telling him: "The Tribe of Daws has refused to accept Islam. You should pronounce a curse upon them."
He replied: "O God! Bless the Tribe of Daws with guidance and draw them closer to me." (M)

On being asked whether a Muslim should maintain ties with his non-Muslim mother, the Prophet ﷺ said, "Yes, you should fulfil your obligations towards her and treat her well." (M)

It is not bigotry to love one's own community. Prejudice and unfairness, however, lies in supporting one's community even in its wrong and unjust acts. (A/I)

Even if a part of one's income is unlawful, his prayer is not accepted by God. (A)

When Asma, a Companion, sought the Prophet's advice as to how she should treat her unbelieving mother, who was visiting her, he told her to take good care of her and help her out financially if she needed it. (B)

God will show mercy to he who is lenient and polite in his business transactions, especially in demanding the repayment of a loan. (B)

Of all the commitments you make, the most serious one, which should be fulfilled promptly, is the payment of the dower to your wife. It is the dower which sanctifies your sexual relations with her. (B/M)

All of Adam's children are liable to err; however, the best of them are those who repent after having sinned. (T)

The one characterized by the following traits will be blessed with a peaceful death: (i) leniency towards the weak; (ii) love and respect for parents; and (iii) taking good care of one's dependants. (BQ)

The one who wants that his sustenance be enlarged and that he may enjoy a long life should treat his relatives well and do favours for them. (B/M)

Under Islamic governance, Muslims pledge to protect the lives, property and honour of all non-Muslim citizens. If anyone wrongs them, deprives them of their rights, oppresses them or usurps their property, I [the Prophet Muhammad ﷺ] will take up these victims' case in God's court. (D)

Do not run after a good position: if you do so, you will fail to discharge your duty. However, if a position of responsibility is assigned to you, then God will help and support you. (B/M)

Whoever does not abuse his tongue or his private parts is guaranteed to enter Paradise. (B)

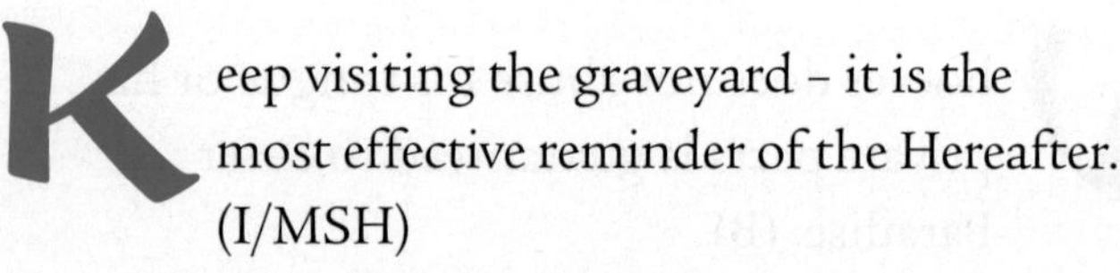

Keep visiting the graveyard – it is the most effective reminder of the Hereafter. (I/MSH)

While drinking water, do not gulp it down in one go. Rather, take small sips. As you start drinking, say, “In the name of God, Most Compassionate, Most Merciful”, and, when you finish, say, “Praise be to God”. (T)

What should we say when we face a problem: "God is enough for us, and He is the best Guardian and Helper." (B)

If one borrows money with the intention to repay it, yet he is unable to do so, God will enable him to repay it somehow. However, if he did not mean to repay it in the first place, God will destroy him for his evil intention. (B)

None of you will die before getting all the sustenance that God has already decreed for you. Fear God and employ only fair means in getting your daily bread. Any delay in securing your sustenance should not prompt you to use unfair means. You can only get what is with God through your obedience to Him. (MSH)

Here is the way to endear yourself to God and to people: shun materialism and worldliness, and God will love you. Become indifferent to the wealth of others, and it will endear them to you. (T/I)

Saying a good word is equal to giving in charity. (B)

od showers His mercy upon those who are kind and considerate towards their fellow human beings. (B)

O humanity, listen! Your Lord is One and Adam is your father. No Arab is superior to a non-Arab. Nor is any non-Arab superior to an Arab. No white person is better than a black one. Nor is any black person better than a white one. Your superiority is only on the basis of piety. (A)

Do you not fear God regarding the animal He places in your care? Neither keep it hungry nor overburden it with hard work. (M)

Help your brother, whether he is the victim or the oppressor. Helping the oppressor means dissuading him from being unjust to anyone. (M/MSH)

The body fed on unlawful earnings is unfit for Paradise: it is only fit for the Hellfire. (A/BQ)

On the death of the son of his Companion, Mu'adh, the Prophet ﷺ sent him the following note of condolence:

In the name of God, Most Compassionate, Most Merciful. All praise be to God, besides Whom there is no god. I pray that God shower His rewards upon you for the loss you have suffered. May He grant you peace of mind and heart. May He enable us and you to thank Him for His innumerable blessings. The truth is that our lives, our belongings and our families are precious gifts from Him; these are trusts placed with us. Your son too was one of His blessings granted to you. As long as this blessing pleased Him, He let you enjoy it. As He willed,

He recalled it. You are nonetheless destined to receive a big reward for this loss. I give you glad tidings of His special mercy, if your bear patiently with this loss to earn His pleasure and reward. O Mu'adh! Be patient lest your lamentation wipe out your reward. It would render you all the poorer and more regretful. Remember that your mourning can neither bring back the dead nor can it relieve your loss and suffering. God's command is bound to prevail. His will has already been accomplished. Peace and blessings be upon you! (TB)

The one who declines an invitation to a meal without a valid reason is guilty of having disobeyed God and His Messenger. By contrast, an uninvited person who gatecrashes into a feast is as wicked as a burglar. (D/MSH)

The one guilty of severing ties of kinship will not be admitted to Paradise. (B/M)

God will not disclose the failings of he who refrains from speaking ill of others. He who controls his anger will be protected from His anger on the Day of Judgement. He who pleads guilty to Him for his sins will be pardoned by Him. (BQ)

Offering a good, kind word is an act of charity that entitles one to God's reward. (B)

The best among people is he who is the most pious, Godfearing and truthful. His conduct is not tainted by any sin, injustice, jealousy or rancour. (I/BQ)

The one who is untrustworthy is devoid of faith. The one who does not keep his word stands outside the fold of faith. (BQ)

He is not strong who can defeat anyone in a wrestling bout; rather, mighty is he who controls himself even in a fit of anger. (M/MSH)

Anyone taking pains to help a widow or a poor, needy person is like one who strives in God's way. He is as praiseworthy as one who worships throughout the night, without complaining of fatigue, or as one who observes consecutive fasts. (B/M)

The one who does not thank his benefactor is ungrateful to God. (A/T)

If you know a truly pious person who does not indulge in vain talk and keeps away from worldliness, you should keep his company. God bestows wisdom upon such a pious person. (BQ)

Shun suspicion and conjecture: suspicion is based on falsehood. (MSH)

Before entering someone's house, seek permission. You should go away if permission is not granted. (D)

If one goes to bed with the intention of getting up early to offer the pre-dawn prayer but fails to do so because of oversleeping, then one will still be credited with having performed that prayer. His oversleeping will be condoned by the Lord out of His grace and affection. (N/I)

One adopts the way of his friend, so be careful in selecting your friends. (A)

Do not incur a victim's curse upon you for his supplication reaches God directly. God detests that anyone be oppressed. (MSH)

DAY 320

Your pious friend is like a bearer of musk, for at least you would be blessed with fragrance in his company. On the other hand, your wicked, evildoing friend is like an ironsmith at work, whose company is bound to contaminate you. (MSH)

The one who is blessed with the following will enjoy the best of both the worlds: (i) a heart overflowing with gratitude to God; (ii) a tongue consistently engaged in the remembrance of God; (iii) a temperament to tolerate loss and suffering; and (iv) a sincere and loyal spouse. (BQ/MSH)

The marriage feast to which only the rich are invited while excluding the poor is detestable. (B/M)

The following are some of the major sins: (i) to associate anyone with God in His divinity; (ii) to disobey parents; (iii) to kill anyone; and (iv) to tell a lie. (M)

Pay a worker his wages promptly – even before he stops perspiring. (I)

O Lord! I seek refuge in You against hardship, sorrow, inaction and laziness, the burdens of debt and the influence of evil people. (B/M)

God overlooks the lapses of a person who does not speak ill of others. Likewise, whoever controls his anger will be protected from God's punishment on the Day of Judgement. And whoever pleads guilty before God will have his plea accepted. (BQ)

On appointing Mu‘adh as governor of the Yemen, the Prophet ﷺ advised him, “Keep away from a life of luxury. God’s chosen servants do not lead a life of ease and comfort.” (A)

If you pledge to observe the following, I assure you entry into Paradise: (i) whenever you say something, speak the truth; (ii) whenever you make a promise, keep your word; (iii) whenever something is placed in your trust, guard it and return it; (iv) do not abuse your private parts; (v) avoid even looking at what is forbidden; and (vi) exercise self-restraint by neither harming nor depriving anyone of their due. (A/BQ)

Do not speak ill of the dead. They are already with their Lord and will be recompensed according to their deeds. (AM)

hoever among you is capable of helping another, you should do so. (M)

To remove an obstacle from the path that may inconvenience people is an act of charity. (B)

O servants of God! Be brothers to one another. All believers are part of the same fraternity. A believer does not wrong a fellow believer, nor does he leave him in the lurch: (i) do not look down upon others; (ii) do not be jealous of each other; (iii) do not nurse grudges against each other; (iv) do not sever mutual ties; and (v) do not provoke hostility among each other. All this constitutes piety. Evil is he who humiliates a fellow believer. The life, property and honour of a believer are sacred for other believers. (M)

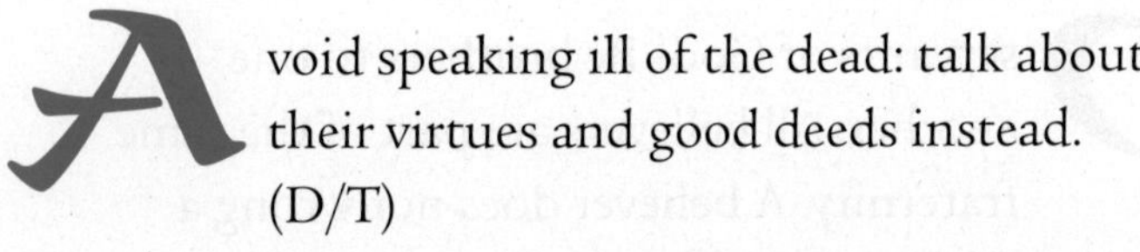

Avoid speaking ill of the dead: talk about their virtues and good deeds instead. (D/T)

Accursed are the one who bribes and the one who accepts it. (D/T)

If you do not accept an apology offered by a fellow Muslim, you will incur God's punishment for your hard-heartedness. (BQ/MSH)

Be discreet in fulfilling your needs as the successful are typically envied. (TB)

A husband should not hate his wife because of something about her which he dislikes: she may have other traits that are pleasing. (M/MSH)

The following types of persons will not be admitted to Paradise: (i) those who cheat people; (ii) those who are miserly; and (iii) those who remind people of the favours they had done them. (TA)

Anyone who travels in the pursuit of knowledge is like he who proceeds towards Paradise. The angels spread their wings, welcoming the seeker of knowledge. All those who are in the heavens and on the earth, including even the fish in the deep waters, pray and seek forgiveness for him. A scholar enjoys superiority over a worshipper like the full moon does over the stars. (D)

The odour from the mouth of a fasting person is more agreeable to God than the fragrance of musk. (M)

A single religious scholar gifted with understanding and tact is far more effective in thwarting Satan's mischief than a large number of devout and naïve worshippers. (T/MSH)

Someone sought the Prophet's permission to join the Jihad (fighting in God's way). He asked him whether his mother was alive. When he affirmed it, he directed him to stay at home and take care of her. The Prophet ﷺ concluded his directive thus: "Go and look after her. Paradise lies at the feet of your mother." (A/N/BQ)

God may pardon any sin. However, He has decreed that anyone guilty of disobedience to his parents will face punishment in this world. (MSH)

The one who gossips cannot enter Paradise. (B/M)

The way to Paradise is marked by self-restraint while the gratification of base desire leads straight to Hell. (MSH)

O God! I seek Your protection from cowardice, lethargy and laziness. I seek Your refuge against excessive old age, debt, Hellfire and punishment in Hell, the torment and punishment of the grave, the evils of affluence and poverty, and against hard-heartedness, negligence, impoverishment, humiliation and helplessness. I seek Your refuge against unbelief, obstinacy, showing off, deafness, dumbness, madness, leprosy and all tormenting diseases. I seek Your protection against the burden of debt, worry, sorrow, miserliness, indignity and overripe old age. (I)

'Aishah, the Prophet's wife, reports that throughout his life the Prophet ﷺ never took revenge on personal grounds. However, he only exacted justice in cases involving the violation of God's commands. (B/M)

For a newly-wedded couple: May God bless you, lavish His bounties on you and keep you together in all that is good and blessed. (A/MSH)

Do not be immoderate in praising me. Do not be like the Christians who have gone too far in extolling Jesus, son of Mary. I am merely a servant of God. Regard me only as a servant and Messenger of God. (B/M)

You may protect yourselves against God's wrath befalling you, provided you treat inarticulate, dumb animals kindly. Ride them only so long as they are fit, and give them proper rest at the end of a journey. (D)

People only get the rulers that befit them. (MSH)

When you finish eating and drinking, say, "Praise be to God Who provided us with food and drink and made us believers." (T/D)

There will come a time when people will be wholly indifferent as to whether their income is lawful or not. (B)

On being faced with loss and suffering, one should not wish for death. If one is unable to bear the pain one may, at most, offer the following supplication: "O Lord! Keep me alive as long as it is good for me and cause me to die when it is better for me." (B/MSH)

A Bedouin visiting a mosque for the first time urinated inside and those present scolded him. However, the Prophet ﷺ intervened, saying, "Leave him alone. Pour some water and wash the floor. You are here to make life easy for everyone. You should not cause hardship to anyone." (B)

It is far better for you that you collect wood in the forest and sell it to get bread rather than begging for food. (I/A)

O God! I seek from You wholesome sustenance, beneficial knowledge and such deeds as You accept. (TB)

One should not seek favours from fellow human beings. If one drops something while riding, he ought to get off and pick it up, rather than ask someone else to do it for him. (T)

Keep exchanging presents among yourselves – it removes any ill feeling that you may have for one another. (T)

A prayer for all occasions: O Lord, I ask You to help me accomplish what is good and leave what is bad, and to have love for the poor and needy, and I ask You to forgive me and have mercy on me. I ask You for Your love, and for the love of those who love You, and for the love of deeds that will draw me closer to Your love. (B)

My Lord, have mercy on my parents, as they did care for me when I was little. (Qur'an)

You will soon lust after power, coveting worldly rank. This will only bring disgrace upon you on the Day of Judgement. (D)

od accepts a man's repentance even when he is on the verge of death. (T)

O God! Make my inner state better than my outer one and make me pious outwardly as well. I seek from You such good things as You grant – wealth, wives and children. Protect me from going astray. Let me not mislead anyone. (T)

The best among you are those who have excellent character and conduct. (B/M)

INDEX

All references refer to page numbers.